MW01130195

Amazing Animals

Strange Animal Partnerships

Multiplying Fractions

Jay Hwang

Consultants

Michele Ogden, Ed.D
Principal
Irvine Unified School District

Colleen Pollitt, M.A.Ed.
Math Support Teacher
Howard County Public Schools

Publishing Credits

Rachelle Cracchiolo, M.S.Ed., *Publisher*
Conni Medina, M.A.Ed., *Managing Editor*
Dona Herweck Rice, *Series Developer*
Emily R. Smith, M.A.Ed., *Series Developer*
Diana Kenney, M.A.Ed., NBCT, *Content Director*
Stacy Monsman, M.A., *Editor*
Kevin Panter, *Graphic Designer*

Image Credits: Cover and pp.1, 27 Juniors Bildarchiv GmbH/Alamy Stock Photo; pp.10–11 F1online digitale Bildagentur GmbH/Alamy Stock Photo; p.11 (bottom) Daniel L. Geiger/SNAP/Alamy Stock Photo; p.20 Stocktrek Images, Inc./Alamy Stock Photo; all other images from iStock and/or Shutterstock.

Library of Congress Cataloging-in-Publication Data

Names: Hwang, Jay, author.
Title: Strange animal partnerships / Jay Hwang.
Description: Huntington Beach, CA : Teacher Created Materials, [2018] | Series: Amazing animals | Audience: Grade 4 to 6. | Includes index.
Identifiers: LCCN 2017012134 (print) | LCCN 2017014326 (ebook) | ISBN 9781480759374 (eBook) | ISBN 9781425855550 (paperback)
Subjects: LCSH: Symbiosis--Juvenile literature.
Classification: LCC QH548 (ebook) | LCC QH548 .H83 2018 (print) | DDC 577.8/5--dc23
LC record available at https://lccn.loc.gov/2017012134

Teacher Created Materials

5301 Oceanus Drive
Huntington Beach, CA 92649-1030
http://www.tcmpub.com

ISBN 978-1-4258-5555-0

© 2018 Teacher Created Materials, Inc.

Table of Contents

Go, Team Nature!

The great outdoors can be a scary place for any living thing. Wild animals must hunt for food. They also need to stay safe from **predators**. Even one day without food or water can be disastrous. A day without food means less energy to hunt or run. A few days without water and it might be hard to see straight!

Make no mistake; living in the wild is very tough. However, having friends can make life much easier! An **interdependent** relationship can help two living things survive. Both partners in this type of relationship get something good in return. It's sort of like getting paid to mow a neighbor's lawn!

Think about the flowers and bees that you see outside. Flowers on plants give bees nectar to drink, and in return, bees spread pollen to help new plants grow. Both the plants and bees receive something they need from the relationship. It's a win-win situation! Let's look at other examples of these kinds of relationships in nature. Go, Team Nature!

As the bee drinks nectar, pollen sticks to its body.

Masters of Disguise

Some creatures disguise themselves to hide from danger. The decorator crab is a great example of a disguise artist. These crabs live in shallow waters, which makes it easy for predators to spot them. They hide themselves with things from their environment. One thing decorator crabs use are sea sponges.

There are more than 5,000 **species** of sea sponges. They come in a variety of colors, shapes, and sizes. If a large sea sponge breaks, it becomes two smaller sea sponges! To survive, sea sponges **filter** water to find food. Sea sponges could find more food if they could move. Unfortunately, they can't walk around on their own. A sea sponge could use a good friend!

Decorator crabs and sea sponges have an interdependent relationship. Decorator crabs pick up sea sponges and place them on their backs. By doing so, sea sponges hide crabs from the sight of predators. In return, crabs move sponges around and offer them new places to feed. Now that's great teamwork!

Imagine a small sea sponge is about $\frac{1}{3}$ the size of a decorator crab. How many decorator crabs can 6 sea sponges cover? Draw a model to show your thinking.

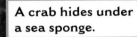

A crab hides under a sea sponge.

decorator crab

7

Look and Listen

Zebras are striped animals found on the African plains. They grow to be 3 feet (1 meter) to 5 feet (1.5 meters) tall and weigh between 440 pounds (200 kilograms) and 900 pounds (408 kilograms). They are social animals who spend their time in large herds. They graze together on grass and groom one another. Also, their unique stripes blend together with the stripes of other zebras. This appearance confuses predators. Still, zebras must be constantly on guard against lions and hyenas.

Like zebras, ostriches also live in herds in Africa. But, their herds are much smaller. Ostriches are large birds that grow to be 7 ft. (2 m) to 10 ft. (3 m) tall and weigh 220 lbs. (100 kg) to 350 lbs. (159 kg). They cannot fly. But, they are very strong runners. Running helps them escape lions, hyenas, and other predators on the plains.

How are these animals able to help each other? Ostriches have a poor sense of hearing and smell but great eyesight. And, zebras have poor eyesight but a strong sense of smell. Ostriches can see predators coming, and zebras can smell them before they get too close. Together, they keep each other safe.

Zebras and ostriches share space on the African plains.

shrimp goby fish

snapping shrimp

Who's Looking Out for You?

Another interdependent relationship can be seen between a snapping shrimp and a shrimp goby fish. Snapping shrimps dig holes to hide in on the seafloor. The holes protect them from predators that want to eat their soft, white bodies. But, snapping shrimps have weaknesses. They have very poor eyesight. Deep holes help, but they are not enough to protect the shrimp from predators they cannot see.

Enter the shrimp goby! This fish has better eyesight than the snapping shrimp. At 4 inches (10 centimeters) long, it is about double the size of the shrimp. But, it is not able to dig its own home. So, the goby lives in the hole made by the snapping shrimp. In return, the goby keeps watch just outside of the hole. When the goby spots predators, it moves its fin, tail, or body. This sends a signal to the shrimp that threats are near. The shrimp uses its long antennae to stay in contact with the goby, so it always gets the message.

These animal partners usually do not move very far. With the shrimp goby keeping a lookout, the snapping shrimp is free to dig a home for both of them without worry.

LET'S EXPLORE MATH

Suppose a snapping shrimp is $\frac{1}{6}$ foot long. It digs a hole in the sand that is 6 times its length. How deep is the hole? Show your thinking.

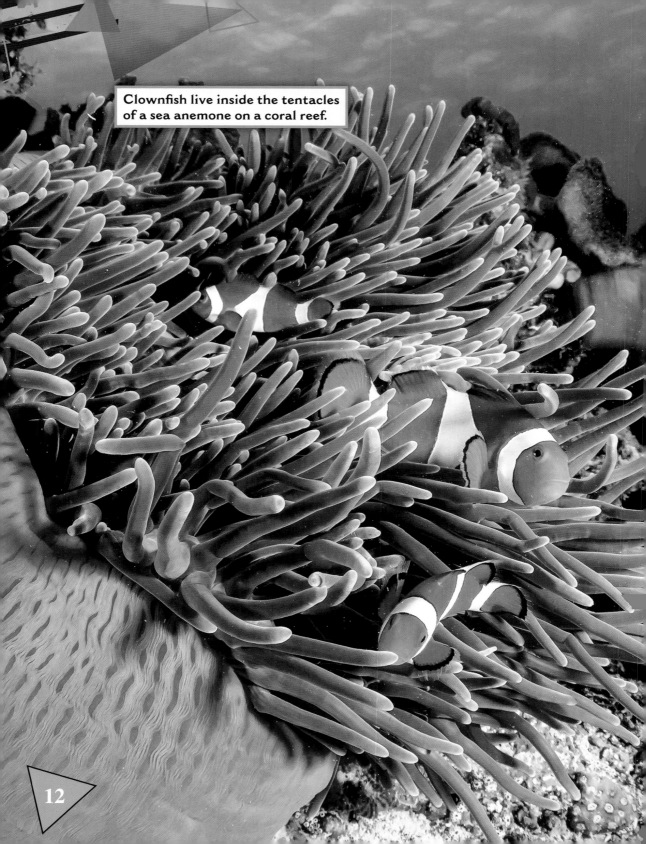

Clownfish live inside the tentacles of a sea anemone on a coral reef.

Home Sweet Home

Sea anemones (uh-NEM-uh-nees) look like pom-poms dropped on the ocean floor. They come in many colors, including yellow, green, and blue. They range in size from a fraction of an inch to 6 ft. (2 m) in length. A sea anemone has many tentacles. Each tentacle has a stinger, which it uses to catch **prey**. The sea anemone sticks to the surface it is on, so it must wait for its prey to pass by.

Clownfish are one of the few fish that nest inside sea anemones. They have orange, white, and black stripes. They can grow up to 4 in. (10 cm) in length. Clownfish are **territorial**. They scare away other fish that come too close to their homes. Amazingly, the stinging tentacles of sea anemones do not hurt clownfish.

Sea anemones and clownfish have a special relationship. They protect each other from many predators. Sea anemones sting fish that eat clownfish, and clownfish scare away fish that eat sea anemones. Looks like these two will be best friends for a long time!

LET'S EXPLORE MATH

Imagine a young sea anemone is $\frac{1}{2}$ foot long. As an adult, it grows 3 times as long. How long will the sea anemone be as an adult? Draw and use a number line like the one below to show 3 jumps of $\frac{1}{2}$.

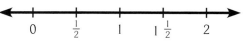

0    $\frac{1}{2}$ 1 $1\frac{1}{2}$ 2

Two wrasses clean a puffer fish.

A puffer fish inflates to defend itself.

fourline wrasse

Time to Visit the Dentist

Wrasses are known as the Dentists of the Sea. These fish eat **parasites** and waste that other fish have trouble getting rid of on their own. Wrasses clean groupers, eels, snappers, and many other fish.

There are nearly 500 species of wrasse. They are very colorful and have smooth scales. They are usually small in size; many are about 8 in. (20 cm) long. But, some wrasses can grow more than 7 ft. (2 m) in length.

Puffer fish can inflate themselves with water or air. They can turn into spiky balls when threatened. Puffer fish have a **toxin** inside their spikes that can cause death. One puffer fish has enough poison to kill up to 30 people!

Puffer fish need to be cleaned and wrasses are there to help. They eat parasites off puffer fish. But, one wrong move and a wrasse could die. Despite this, wrasses continue to provide cleaning services to puffer fish. In exchange for ridding them of parasites, the wrasses eat as often as they like.

Nowhere to Hide

Groupers are large fish that live and hunt in warm seas. They are normally green or brown. Some groupers, such as the Nassau grouper, can change color and patterns. Groupers are bulky. Goliath groupers can grow up to 9 ft. (3 m) long and weigh up to 800 pounds! Due to their size, they are unable to catch prey that hides in rocks or coral reefs. Therefore, they hunt for food in the open ocean where there is no place for prey to hide. Groupers are **diurnal** (dahy-UR-nl) predators, which means they hunt during the day.

Like groupers, moray eels also live in warm seas. They have long, slender bodies with powerful jaws and sharp teeth. Most moray eels grow up to 5 ft. (2 m) in length. Unlike groupers, moray eels are **nocturnal** predators, which means they hunt at night.

So, how do groupers and moray eels help each other? Groupers hunt prey that moray eels chase out of rocks and coral reef. Moray eels trap prey that groupers chase into rocks and coral reef. As a result of their 24-hour teamwork, their prey have nowhere to hide!

A grouper and a moray eel work together to hunt.

A tickbird eats pests from a giraffe's body.

Friends in High Places

The tickbird is a small, brown bird that can grow up to 8 in. (20 cm) long. Tickbirds have either red or yellow beaks. They help to improve the health of animals. They sit on top of oxen, cattle, and other large animals and eat small pests such as ticks, flies, and maggots. Not only that, tickbirds alert other animals of danger by making loud hissing noises.

Giraffes are the tallest of all land mammals and can grow up to 18 ft. (5 m) in height. Giraffes use their height and long tongues to eat leaves that are high in the trees. Small pests such as ticks and maggots can infest their skin. And, it's not easy for a giraffe to get rid of these pests.

An unexpected friend of a giraffe is a tickbird. Tickbirds eat pests from giraffes' bodies. At the same time, giraffes provide tickbirds with a convenient source of food. Not to mention, a great place to rest their wings!

LET'S EXPLORE MATH

A flock of tickbirds flies over a group of giraffes. Of this flock, $\frac{2}{10}$ land on one giraffe. Four times as many tickbirds land on a second giraffe. What fraction of the flock landed on the second giraffe? Complete the equation to show the solution.

$$4 \times \frac{2}{10} = \frac{\Box}{\Box} + \frac{\Box}{\Box} + \frac{\Box}{\Box} + \frac{\Box}{\Box} = \frac{\Box}{\Box}$$

Remoras attach to a shipwreck's hull off the coast of Fiji.

Stuck on You

Remoras are thin, dark fish that live in warm waters. They can grow up to 3 ft. (1 m) long. Remoras are also called "suckerfish" because they use suction cups on their heads to attach to sharks. Some even attach themselves to ships and scuba divers!

Remoras don't have any trouble finding sharks to latch onto. There are more than 400 living species of sharks. The whale shark is the largest fish in the world and can reach lengths of up to 59 ft. (18 m). That is longer than a school bus! Some sharks, like the whale shark and basking shark, eat **plankton**. Other sharks, like the great white shark and Greenland shark, eat other fish, seals, and sea turtles.

Remoras assist sharks by eating **bacteria** and small pests that are harmful to them. This keeps sharks healthy. In turn, remoras get to eat the shark's leftover food, which keeps them full and satisfied. But, remoras must hang on tight since sharks won't think twice before having them for lunch if given the opportunity!

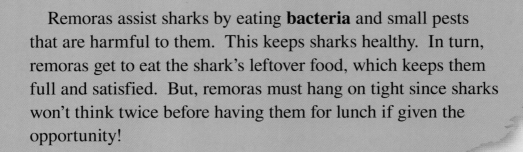

Remoras hitch a ride on a lemon shark.

LET'S EXPLORE MATH

Suppose there are 5 remoras that are each $\frac{3}{8}$ meter long. How many meters long are the remoras in all? Show your thinking.

Wash Me!

The banded mongoose is a small mammal with a bold personality. It has distinct dark brown stripes on its back. Some species of mongoose live alone. Banded mongooses, however, live in large groups. They live in holes that they dig in the ground. They eat small animals, insects, and fruit.

A friend of the banded mongoose is the warthog. Warthogs are a species of wild pig with large, bony tusks and long, thin tails. Their tusks can grow longer than 2 ft. (60 cm). They use their tusks to defend themselves from other animals. Warthogs can even defend themselves against larger predators, such as lions. Despite their fierce appearance, they are social animals that eat grass and other plants.

A banded mongoose and a warthog are very compatible. A banded mongoose acts as a cleaning crew to a warthog. It eats ticks off a warthog's skin while it rests. In the end, the warthog receives a good grooming, and the banded mongoose gets a tasty treat!

A banded mongoose cleans a warthog's skin.

Sweet Dreams

Although people may think ants are annoying, they can be very helpful to some insects. There are about 10,000 species of ants. They live all around the world but are more common in hot areas. Ants can range from $\frac{2}{25}$ inch (2 millimeters) to 1 inch (25 millimeters) in size. In a **colony**, there are three types of ants: the queen, the males, and the workers. Queens lay the eggs, males mate with the queen, and workers gather food for the colony.

The scale insect is an ant's best friend. Scale insects have pale green bodies covered by waxy shells. Their shells look like cotton and help them stick to plants. Scale insects use their straw-like mouths to drink sap from plants. As they drink, they secrete waste in the form of sweet droppings called honeydew.

The honeydew secreted by scale insects provides ants with sugar to eat. In return, ants protect scale insects from predators. When water is scarce, the sugar stored in plants becomes even sweeter. This makes the scale insect's honeydew more sugary, which attracts more ants. Just like many people, ants are very fond of sweets!

An ant feeds on honeydew secreted by a group of scale insects.

Studying Animal Relationships

We all benefit from relationships in some way. Take your best friend, for instance. It could be a classmate, your brother or sister, or even your dog. In the case of a dog, you fulfill all of your dog's needs. You give your dog food, water, and shelter. You keep your dog healthy. In return, your dog gives you endless love. The feelings are definitely mutual!

Just like humans, animals rely on each other, too. What would you think if you saw a little plover bird hop toward the mouth of a crocodile? By now, you might guess that the two animals help each other in some way. You're now thinking like a scientist who studies animal relationships. Can you think of other animals that might benefit from each other? Maybe you will be the one to make the next animal discovery!

A plover cleans a crocodile's teeth and gets a free meal in return.

⚙️ Problem Solving

Imagine you are a marine biologist. You are studying interdependent relationships between animals that live at an aquarium. You are measuring the lengths of the animals to see whether their sizes have any bearing on their relationships.

1. You measure a snapping shrimp. It is $\frac{1}{6}$ foot long. Its companion, a shrimp goby fish, is twice the length. How long is the goby?

2. A clownfish is $\frac{1}{10}$ meter long. Its trusted friend, a sea anemone, is 10 times longer. How long is the sea anemone?

3. A puffer fish is $\frac{2}{5}$ yard long. Its loyal buddy, a wrasse, is 3 times as long. How long is the wrasse?

4. A remora fish is $\frac{2}{3}$ yard long. Its pal, a shark, is 9 times as long. How long is the shark?

5. Look at the lengths of the animals that have interdependent relationships. Do you think their sizes have any influence on their relationships? Why or why not?

Glossary

bacteria—microscopic living things that may be beneficial to animals or may cause infections or disease

colony—a group of plants or animals growing or living in one area

diurnal—active mostly during the day

filter—to remove something from a liquid or gas that passes through it

interdependent—existing between two things that depend on each other

nocturnal—active mostly during the night

parasites—animals or plants that live in or on another organism and benefit from it

plankton—small organisms and plant life in a body of water

predators—animals that kill and eat other animals

prey—animals that are hunted and killed

species—groups of animals or plants that are similar and can produce young

territorial—protective of land from intruders

toxin—a poisonous substance produced by a living thing

Index

Answer Key

Let's Explore Math

page 7:

2 decorator crabs; Possible model:

$\frac{1}{3}$	$\frac{1}{3}$	$\frac{1}{3}$

$\frac{1}{3}$	$\frac{1}{3}$	$\frac{1}{3}$

page 11:

$6 \times \frac{1}{6} = \frac{6}{6}$ or 1 foot

page 13:

$3 \times \frac{1}{2} = \frac{3}{2}$ or $1\frac{1}{2}$ feet; Number line should show 3 jumps of $\frac{1}{2}$ with the last jump landing on $1\frac{1}{2}$.

page 19:

$4 \times \frac{2}{10} = \frac{2}{10} + \frac{2}{10} + \frac{2}{10} + \frac{2}{10} = \frac{8}{10}$ or $\frac{4}{5}$ of the flock

page 21:

$5 \times \frac{3}{8} = \frac{15}{8}$ or $1\frac{7}{8}$ meters

Problem Solving

1. $2 \times \frac{1}{6} = \frac{2}{6}$ or $\frac{1}{3}$ foot
2. $10 \times \frac{1}{10} = \frac{10}{10}$ or 1 meter
3. $3 \times \frac{2}{5} = \frac{6}{5}$ or $1\frac{1}{5}$ yards
4. $9 \times \frac{2}{3} = \frac{18}{3}$ or 6 yards
5. Answers will vary, but should include that the length of the animals has no influence on their interdependent relationship. While some animals in this type of relationship are close in size, the size of one animal can be much larger than its partner.